JN426835

WORDS TO LIVE BY

HELPING #4

Nahm-Sheik Park

국제영어대학원대학교 출판부
INTERNATIONAL GRADUATE SCHOOL OF ENGLISH PRESS

To Joseph Hun Kwak (1941-2011)

from here to eternity

Contents

Preface

This is the youngest 'quadruplet' in the WORDS TO LIVE BY series and follows the footsteps of its three older 'siblings' already out in print. Intended as a 'cup of joe' for Korean students of English, the current compilation also will hopefully help keep in tiptop shape their command of both the language and the innermost reaches of their souls. The adages comprising this collection have been selected for the natural English idiom and soul-enriching bits of thought they come wrapped in.

The volume is small for a purpose: it is designed to conveniently fit into a pocket or purse. The 'petite' size should make it easier for those on the go to carry it around. They will find it chock full of gems of wit, a glimpse of which is readily available on every single page. Thus the current serving of WORDS TO LIVE BY should prove to be another welcome companion to, say, Korea's time-pressed, English-loving commuters. That said, size does indeed matter here, which should give a whole new meaning to "The best things come in small packages" and "Small is beautiful."

The proverbs featured here have all sort of "stood the test of time" at IGSE (International Graduate School of English). They have already received a warm and fuzzy hug at home on the IGSE intranet from students, alums, faculty and staff alike.

If its three predecessors are any guide, the current serving of WORDS TO LIVE BY is likely to meet with just as warm a reception from outside IGSE as well.

The author is delighted to present this booklet as one more face of IGSE, of which he has been president over the last five years. The wish is to help afford IGSE a long-overdue and well-deserved introduction to the broader Korean society. For now, the school boasts a fairly impressive ELT resume as a unique incubator of topnotch teachers of English for the country. IGSE's programs in teacher training are touted to be among Korea's very best.

My thanks go to Ms. Jungmin Choi for the superb editing touches she has put on the book. Ms. Songwon Kim has once again offered pro bono service to grace this publication with yet another one-of-a-kind cover design. I take great pleasure in acknowledging my debt of gratitude to both these ladies, whose contributions have added plenty of luster to the final product. Last but not least, I am also indebted to Mr. Hyeonil Shin, whose word-processing service came in handy in the preparation of the draft for this fourth serving of WORDS TO LIVE BY.

12 August 2011
Nahm-Sheik Park

1

A good beginning makes a good ending.

A good start matters a whole lot especially when it comes to major undertakings. It's not for nothing that they say "Well begun is half done" and "The first blow is half the battle."

• matter a whole lot: 매우 중요하다 • undertaking: 과업, 일 • not for nothing: 그럴만한 이유가 있는 • blow: 타격, 가격

2

The wolf may lose his teeth, but never his nature.

A villain is a villain is a villain. Human nature is immutable by and large. This may especially be the case when it comes to undesirable traits like a mean streak.

• X is X is X: X는 어쩔 수 없는 X이다 • immutable: 변하지 않는 • by and large: 일반적으로 • mean streak: 악한 성격

3

Contempt will sooner kill an injury than revenge.

The best way to get even is not to get even at all. When insulted, for example, don't say or do anything. An act of injustice may indeed be beneath contempt.

• contempt: 경멸, 무시 • revenge: 복수 • get even: 앙갚음하다 • beneath contempt: 경멸할 가치도 없는

4

Point not at others' spots with a foul finger.

Far from "spotless"ourselves, we all make mistakes now and then. Given this fact of life, shouldn't we always think twice about pointing the finger at other people?

• far from spotless: 무결점과는 거리가 먼 • now and then: occasionally, 이따금
• given X: in light of X, X에 비추어 보면 • think twice about X: X를 재고하다
• point the finger at X: X를 손가락질하다

5

Come not to counsel uncalled.

Think twice before giving out counsel. Advice is often unwanted and thus anything but welcome no matter how well-meaning it may be. Kibitzing is Exhibit A.

• counsel uncalled: 상대방이 원치도 않는 조언을 하다 • think twice before X: X를 신중히 생각하다 • well-meaning: 좋은 의도에서 나온 • kibitz: 훈수하다, 참견하다 • Exhibit A: 보기, 증거

6

Content is more than a kingdom.

The world is his that is content with what little he has. All happiness being in the mind, such a person would have nothing to envy. Not even a whole kingdom.

• content with X: X에 만족하는 • what little X has: (조금이라도) X가 이미 가지고 있는 것 • be in the mind: 생각하기 나름이다, 내적인 문제이다

7

Crowns have cares.

A position of (supreme) authority is not necessarily a bed of roses. It is often a bed of brambles. Unwieldy issues have a way of coming with the territory.

• Crowns have cares: 왕관을 쓰면 근심거리가 생긴다 • bed of roses: 편안한 (잠)자리 • bed of brambles: 불편한 (잠)자리 • unwieldy: 다루기 힘든 • have a way of coming with the territory: 으레 따라다니는 자리세이다, 자리에 따라다니는 문제이다

8

Better be alone than in bad company.

The advice here is to keep from hanging out with a bad gang. This axiom apparently helps explain why solitude is often said to be the best society.

• keep from X: X를 삼가다 • hang out with X: X와 어울려 다니다 • bad gang: 불량배 집단 • solitude: 고독 • the best society: 가장 좋은 벗

9

Handsome is as handsome does.

What really matters is deeds, not looks or words. "Pretty is as pretty does" is another way of saying the same thing. In either version, "as" may be replaced by "that."

• Handsome is as handsome does: 하는 짓이 예뻐야 예쁘다 • What really matters: 정말 중요한 것 • in either version: 두 표현 가운데 어느 쪽이건

10

Evil to him who evil thinks

A pox on all who harbor evil thoughts. Evil minds will get their just desserts sooner or later. And evil doers and thinkers deserve whatever grief they may come to.

• Evil to him who evil thinks: 나쁜 짓을 하는 자는 상응하는 벌을 받을지어다 • A pox on X: X는 천벌을 받을지어다 • harbor evil thoughts: 사악한 생각을 하다 • get one's just desserts: 마땅히 받아야 할 벌을 받다 • come to grief: 재앙을 당하다

11

Character is destiny.

Character has a very strong grip that is anything but easy to shake. The way we are will find its way into our life's arc one way or another, leaving an indelible mark behind.

• Character is destiny: 성격은 운명이다 • have a strong grip: 장악력이 강하다 • find one's way into X: X 속으로 들어가다 • life's arc: 인생의 궤적 • one way or another: 어떤 방법으로든지 • indelible: 지울 수 없는

12

Health is not valued till sickness comes.

Only when we get sick do we begin to appreciate what good health is worth. Having said that, shouldn't we put a premium on always staying fit and leave no room for sickness to touch us?

• appreciate X: X의 가치를 인식하다 • Having said that: 그렇다면 • put a premium on X: X를 중요시하다 • stay fit: 건강을 잘 유지하다 • leave no room for X: X가 들어설 여지를 조금도 남겨 두지 않다

13

Stolen waters are sweet.

Forbid a thing, and that people will do. What is forbidden tends to be tempting. In fact, it is often fiendishly irresistible. "Forbidden fruit is sweet" makes a similar point.

• forbid: 금지하다 • tempting: 유혹을 느끼게 하는 • fiendishly: 지독하게 • irresistible: 유혹을 감당할 수 없는

14

There is nothing new under the sun.

We often find ourselves bragging about us doing something groundbreaking. All we are doing may just be re-inventing the wheel, though. It may merely be something old becoming new again.

• brag: 자랑하다 • groundbreaking: 새 분야를 개척하는 • reinvent the wheel: 이미 존재하는 것을 (불필요하게) 다시 만들다 • Something old becomes new again: The wheel gets reinvented

15

Gluttony kills more than the sword.

Greedy eaters dig their graves with their teeth, as they say. When it comes to gluttony, literal or otherwise, a little too much is often much too much.

• gluttony: (지나친) 식탐, 폭음, 폭식 • literal or otherwise: 문자 그대로이건 아니건 • a little too much: 조금 지나치게 많이 • much too much: 너무 지나치게 많이

16

Plain dealing is a jewel.

Integrity is probably the brightest jewel in the crown of human decency. Be aboveboard and you will go far, earning the respect of everyone around you.

• plain dealing: 정직한 거래, 속임수를 쓰지 않음 • be a jewel: 소중하다
• human decency: 인간다움, 인간적인 품위 • aboveboard: 숨김이 없는, 정직한
• go far: 성공하다

17

Nature will have her course.

No one can force nature to change its path. There is nothing we can do about the wrath that nature occasionally wreaks upon us, is there? Take typhoons, for example.

• Nature will have her course: 자연은 정해진 제 길을 간다 • There is nothing we can do about X: X는 어찌할 도리가 없다 • wreak wrath upon X: X에게 분노를 터뜨리다 • occasionally: 이따금 • typhoon: 태풍

18

Lice do not bite busy men.

Keep your nose to the grindstone and there'd be no room for trifles to bother you. Busy men cannot afford the luxury of allowing "lice to bite them," can they?

• Keep your nose to the grindstone: 쉼없이 열심히 일하다 • trifle: 사소한 것
• can afford the luxury of X: X의 여유를 누릴 수 있다

19

Covetousness is always filling a bottomless vessel.

The more you get, the more you want. There is no known boundary to human greed. The sky is the limit. Or is it?

• bottomless vessel: 밑 빠진 그릇 • boundary: 경계 • The sky is the limit: 한정이 없다, 끝이 없다 • Or is it?: 아니, 그 한계가 있던가?

20

Envy eats nothing but its own heart.

Always self-consuming, envy hurts itself the most - far more than it does its target. That being the case, it doesn't have too much to commend it, does it?

• Envy eats nothing but its own heart: 시기/질투는 자신의 심장 만을 파먹을 따름이다 • self-consuming: 자기소모적인 • be the case: be true • X does not have much to commend it: X는 장점이 별로 없다

21

He that is master of himself will soon be master of others.

A great virtue, self-discipline is the mark of a good leader. He is not fit to command others that cannot command himself, is he?

• master of oneself: 스스로를 다스리는 사람 • self-discipline: 자기 절제 • fit: prepared, ready • command onself: 스스로를 다스리다

22

Health is great riches.

Health is indeed worth more than anything in the world. He that wants health wants all, as they say. Health is surely above wealth, isn't it?

• riches: wealth, 부 • want X: X가 결여되다 • as they say: 사람들이 흔히 말하듯 • above X: better than X

23

Homo is a common name to all men.

Humans are basically all the same and thus equal. So, they all deserve treating with equal respect. The sun shines upon all alike, doesn't it?

• homo: 인간 • human: 인간 • treat with equal respect: 동일한 존경심으로 대하다 • The sun shines upon all alike: 태양은 누구에게나 동일하게 비추인다, 누구나 평등하다

24

Soon enough if well enough.

Haste is anything but advisable. How soon something is done doesn't really matter that much, that is, as long as it gets done right. So, make haste slowly.

• Soon enough if well enough: 시간이 걸려도 일이 잘 되면 그만이다
• advisable: 현명한 • that is: that is to say, 즉 • get done right: 제대로 되다
• Make haste slowly: 아무리 급해도 서둘러서는 안된다

25

The belly carries the legs.

We are sustained by what we eat. "An army marches on its stomach" and "Bread is the staff of life" also speak to the importance of our daily bread.

• sustain: 지탱하다 • An army marches on its stomach: 배가 차야 군대가 행군할 수 있다 • Bread is the staff of life: 밥이 인생의 지팡이다 • daily bread: 일용할 양식

26

If cold wind (should) reach you through a hole, say your prayers and mind your soul.

Watch out for a drafty place. Cold wind can give rise to very serious health issues. The air of a window is as the stroke of a crossbow, remember?

• say one's prayers: 기도를 드리다 • mind one's soul: 영혼을 보살피다 • watch out for X: X를 조심하다 • drafty: 바람이 들어오는 • give rise to X: X를 유발시키다 • the stroke of a crossbow: (격발식) 화살에 의한 타격

27

One enemy is too many; a hundred friends too few.

This is a cautionary tale of the danger that an enemy is liable to pose. One enemy can do more harm than can be undone by a hundred friends.

• cautionary tale of X: X에 대한 경고의 메시지 • liable to pose a danger: 위험을 부를 가능성이 있는 • undo X: X를 상쇄하다

28

Drink less and go home by daylight.

In drinking, as in all things else, moderation is king. Temperance may be even better. They say that those who drink a little too much drink much too much.

• by daylight: 해가 지기 전에 • moderation: 절제, 중용 • be king: 제일이다
• temperance: 절제, 금주

29

Four eyes see more than two.

Two people working together can get much more done than just one person working alone. Which is to say that collaboration is good to thrive by.

• Four eyes see more than two: 두 사람(의 네 눈이) 한 사람(의 두 눈) 보다 많이 볼 수 있다 • Which is to say that X: 즉 X, 다시 말해서 X • X is good to thrive by: X는 번창의 좋은 방법이다

30

Familiarity breeds contempt.

Seldom does a hero come across as one to those who are close to him. Proximity may have a way of shrinking the halo of the greatest person (or thing).

• Familiarity breeds contempt: 친근하면 하찮아 보인다 • come across as X: X라는 인상을 주다 • proximity: 근거리 • shrink: 줄이다 • halo: 후광

31

Men do more things through habit than through reason.

Humans are such helpless creatures of habit. We often do things as a matter of habit without even thinking about it. Force of habit may be stronger than force of reason.

• reason: 이성, 합리 • helpless: 무(기)력한 • creature of habit: 습관의 노예 • as a matter of habit: out of habit, through habit, 습관적으로 • force of X: X의 힘

32

Good folks are scarce.

Virtue is a rare commodity. Good people are indeed few and far between. Given the short shrift humanity gets these days, this is far from surprising.

• folks: 사람들 • scarce: 흔하지 않은 • few and far between: scarce, not plentiful • given X: in view of X, in light of X • short shrift: 대수롭지 않게 여김 • humanity: 인간성, 인간다움

33

Early sow, early mow.

The sooner you sow, the sooner you harvest. If you wish to be done early, you should begin early. The early bird catches the worm, doesn't it?

• Early sow, early mow: 빨리 파종하면 빨리 거둔다 • harvest: 수확하다 • be done: be finished • The early bird catches the worm: 아침부터 일찍 활동하는 새가 벌레를 잡는다

34

Night is the mother of counsel.

When you are not sure what to do, take your time and give it a long, hard thought. Sleeping over the whole thing may be the wisest course of action.

• Night is the mother of counsel: 밤이 좋은 조언을 잉태한다 • take one's time: 서두르지 않고 천천히 하다 • give X a long, hard thought: X를 오랫동안 곰곰이 생각하다 • sleep over X: 밤을 새우면서 X를 곰곰이 생각하다 • course of action: 행동 방향

35

Better buy than borrow.

The message here is that we should refrain from borrowing as much as possible. "Neither a borrower nor a lender be" is Shakespeare's way of saying about the same thing.

• refrain from X: X를 삼가다 • Neither a borrower nor a lender be: Be neither a borrower nor a lender

36

Liberty is not license.

Just because we are "free agents" doesn't mean that we can do anything we please. We must stay within bounds of reason, never infringing upon other people's rights to be free.

• Liberty is not license: 자유는 방종이 아니다 • free agent: 자기 마음대로 행동할 수 있는 사람 • stay within bounds of reason: 이성의 한도를 넘지 않다
• infringe upon X: X를 침해하다

37

You can see a mote in another's eye but cannot see a beam in your own.

(Matthews 7:3)

We tend to be much quicker to find fault with other people than with ourselves. Saying the same thing is: "The hunchback doesn't see his own hump but sees his companion's."

• mote: 티끌 • quick to find fault with X: 쉽게 X의 결함을 꼬집다 • hump: 등허리에 난 혹 • companion: 동료, 친구, 상대방

38

Suffering is bitter, but its fruits are sweet.

To reap a harvest of sweet fruits, we must put in endless hours of hard work. No pain(s), no gain(s). The climb to the top is never an easy one, is it?

• reap a harvest of X: X를 수확하다 • put in endless hours of hard work: 수없이 많은 시간에 걸친 고된 일을 하다 • No pain(s), no gain(s): 고통이 없이는, 얻는 것도 없다 • the climb to the top: 최고의 자리에 오르는 것

39

From shirtsleeves to shirtsleeves is only three generations.

Material wealth is not easily handed down from one generation to the next. It just can't be counted on to last long. "Shirtsleeves" here may be replaced by "clogs."

• From shirtsleeves to shirtsleeves is only three generations: 재산은 삼대 이상 대물림할 수 없다 • shirtsleeve: 허름한 옷 • hand down X: X를 물려 주다 • count on X to last long: X가 지속되기를 기대하다 • clog: 나막신

40

Nothing crave, nothing have.

Reach for the stars. There is no motivator quite like a quest for greatness. "Nothing seek, nothing find" also speaks to the value of aspiration.

• Nothing crave, nothing have: 갈망하지 않고는 얻을 수 없다 • reach for the stars: 목표를 높이 세우다 • motivator: 동기를 유발하는 것 • quest for X: X의 추구 • Nothing seek, nothing find: 찾으려 하지 않으면, 찾을 수 없다

41

Good things are theirs that enjoy them.

Take ownership of what the world has to offer you. Enjoy it and be happy. After all, the gown is his that wears it. The choice is all yours.

• take ownership of X: X를 장악하다 • The gown is his that wears it: 가운은 입는 사람이 주인이다 • The choice is all yours: 여러분이 선택하기에 달려 있다

42

There will be sleeping enough in the grave.

The counsel here is against sleeping too much. Sleeping too little can bring serious health issues in its wake, though. Striking a balance is key here.

• There will be sleeping enough in the grave: 죽어서 무덤 속에서도 충분히 잘 수 있다 • The council here is against sleeping too much: 지나치게 많은 수면을 하지 말라는 뜻이다 • bring X in its wake: X를 수반하다 • serious health issues: 심각한 건강문제 • strike a balance: 균형을 취하다 • be key: 중요하다

43

An idle youth, a needy age.

Those who idle away their youth fail to adequately prepare for their old age. We should all try and set aside enough for when old age catches up to us.

• An idle youth, a needy age: 젊어서 게으름 부리면, 늙어서 궁핍해진다 • idle away X: X를 허송하다 • catch up to X: X를 따라 잡다

44

A short prayer penetrates heaven.

We should always deliver our words not by number but by weight. A good prayer doesn't have to be long, does it? And neither does a good essay, right?

• penetrate: 관통하다 • deliver: 전달하다 • not by number but by weight: 수가 아니라 무게로 • essay: 수필, 논문

45

There is one law for the rich and another for the poor.

Everyone should be equal before the law. However, the have-nots apparently are often treated differently in the court of law than the haves are.

• be equal before the law: 법률 앞에 평등하다 • have-nots: 가난한 사람들
• the court of law: 법정 • the haves: 부유한 사람들

46

Where your will is ready, your feet are light.

What is done willingly is done easily. Which should help explain why "one volunteer is worth two pressed men." "Where there is a will, there is a way," right?

• Where your will is ready, your feet are light: 할 의지가 있으면, 발길이 가볍다
• willingly: 하고자 하여 • One volunteer is worth two pressed men: 자발적으로 하는 한 사람이 억지로 하는 두 사람의 몫을 할 수 있다

47

Riches serve a wise man but command a fool.

Money is a good servant but a bad master, right? A similar message applies to other things of value. Power, for example, serves a wise man but commands a fool.

• Riches serve a wise man but command a fool: 재산은 현명한 사람에게는 심부름꾼이지만 바보에게는 그를 부리는 주인이다 • apply to other things of value: 다른 가치 있는 것들에게도 적용된다

48

Better beg than steal.

It is better to be an honest beggar than a disingenuous thief. Integrity should always be our guiding light even when we are in dire need.

• Better beg than steal: 도둑질 보다 구걸이 낫다 • disingenuous: 정직하지 못한 • integrity: 정직 • guiding light: guiding principle, 지표 • dire need: 곤경

49

Who comes late lodges ill.

Laziness is good for naught. It never does anybody any good, does it? The road to failure is often paved with sloth. The early bird catches the worm.

• Who comes late lodges ill: 늦게 오는 사람은 잠자리가 불편하다 • good for naught: 전혀 쓸모가 없다 • never do X any good: X에게 아무런 이득도 되지 못하다 • The road to failure is paved with sloth: 실패에 이르는 길은 게으름으로 포장되어 있다

50

Short pleasure, long repentance.

Let pleasure seekers of the world beware. Worldly pleasure by nature is short-lived and has a long-lasting sting in its tail.

• repentance: 후회 • beware: 주의하다 • worldly pleasure: 세속적인 쾌락 • by nature: 본래, 그 성격상 • have a long-lasting sting it its tail: 꼬리에 오래 지속되는 독침이 있다

51

Hate not at the first harm.

Don't be too quick to hate (others). We must learn not to be too hasty or jumpy in anything we do. Excessive haste is good for nothing.

• Hate not at the first harm: 너무 성급하게 증오하지 말라 • quick to hate: 쉽게 증오하다 • good for nothing: 아무 쓸모 없는

52

Benefits bind.

There is no such thing as a free ride. Once we get something for free, we are beholden to whoever gave it to us. We have to cope with the shackles of their influence.

• Benefits bind: 은혜는 속박을 수반한다 • There is no such thing as a free ride: 무료 승차 같은 것은 존재하지 않는다, 세상에 공짜는 없다 • be beholden to X: X에게 은혜의 빚을 진 • shackles: 족쇄

53

One doctor makes work for another.

The suggestion here is that not all doctors are sufficiently experienced and ethical. That said, we must exercise extra caution when picking a doctor.

• sufficiently: 충분히 • ethical: 윤리적 • exercise extra caution: 각별히 조심하다

54

Nature hates all sudden changes.

It is always best to let nature take its course. Evolution, rather than revolution, should be the route of choice for all reasonable people.

• let X take its course: X의 진로를 방해하지 않고 그대로 놔두다 • evolution: 진화 • revolution: 혁명 • the route of choice: 우선적으로 택하는 길

55

There is no tree but bears some fruit.

Every tree bears fruit of one kind or another, right? By the same token, nothing in the world, however mundane, is without some value or other.

• There is no tree but bears some fruit: 열매를 맺지 않는 나무는 없다 • by the same token: 마찬가지로 • mundane: 하찮은, 세속적인

56

Sometimes the best gain is to lose.

Life is such that gain and loss are the two sides of one and the same coin. No wonder, there is no great loss without some gain and vice versa.

• Sometimes the best gain is to lose: 때로는 잃는 것이 가장 좋은 소득이다
• two sides of the same coin: 같은 동전의 양면 • and vice versa: 그리고 그 반대도 성립한다

57

The footsteps of fortune are slippery.

At any given moment, there is no knowing what the future holds for us. Being fickle and in constant flux, fortune is always liable to catch us off guard.

• slippery: 미끄러지기 쉬운 • there is no Xing: X하는 것이 불가능하다 • what the future holds for X: X의 미래에 어떤 일이 있을지 • fickle: 변덕스러운 • in constant flux: 항상 유동적인

58

Learn weeping and you shall gather laughing.

Learning involves a painful process, but its fruits are sweet. Stay invested in your quest for knowledge. Sweet bundles of joy are sure to come your way.

• Learn weeping and you shall gather laughing: 울면서 어렵게 공부하면 웃으면서 쉽게 거둬들이게 된다 • stay invested in X: X에 공을 들이고 있다 • quest for knowledge: 지식의 추구 • bundle of joy: 한 아름의 즐거움 • come X's way: X에게로 오다

59

Small is beautiful.

We often obsess over how big something is. Size is no reliable gauge of true value, though. Jewels come in small packages, don't they?

• obsess over X: X에 집착하다 • gauge of X: X의 척도 • come in small packages: 조그맣게 포장되어 나오다

60

What goes around comes around.

You reap what you sow. Do something bad to others and it is sure to come back to haunt you. You must face the consequences of what you do.

• What goes around comes around: 돌아 가는 것은 다시 돌아 오게 마련이다
• You reap what you sow: 뿌린 대로 거둔다 • X comes back to haunt Y: X 가 되돌아 와서 Y를 괴롭힌다

61

Hear much, speak little.

Be always attentive, but keep from speaking too much. "From hearing comes wisdom and from speaking repentance" is more explicit about the message implied here.

• be attentive: 남의 말에 귀기울이다 • keep from Xing: X하는 것을 삼가다
• repentance: 후회 • explicit: 명시적, 명백한

62

No man is content with his lot.

No matter how much is already in our possession, we never think we have enough. Our glass is always sort of half empty, isn't it?

• No man is content with his lot: 자기 처지에 만족하는 사람은 없다 • in X's possession: X가 소유하고 있는 • The glass is half empty: 잔이 반밖에 차지 않았다, 처지가 만족스럽지 못하다 • be sort of X: X인 편이다

63

Friendship is a tree which must be often watered.

Friendship doesn't just grow on trees. It must be properly tended. It needs adequate watering and mulching and fertilizing, doesn't it?

• water: 물을 주다 • grow on trees: 거저 생겨나다 • properly: 적절히 • tend: 보살피다 • adequate: 적정한 • mulch: (작물의) 뿌리를 덮개로 덮어 보호하다 • fertilize: 비료를 주다

64

Experience is the best teacher.

There is nothing quite like the school of hard knocks when it comes to learning to do things in life. For example, using English is the best way to learn to use English.

• There is nothing like X: X 이상 좋은 것은 없다 • the school of hard knocks: 어려운 현실 세계

65

Keep your weather-eye open.

Unpredictable as the weather, the world is full of things that need watching out for. Never let your guard down lest you get tripped up by unforeseen things.

• Keep your weather-eye open: 경계를 늦추지 않다 • unpredictable: 예측할 수 없는 • watch out for X: X를 조심하다 • let X's guard down: (X의) 경계를 늦추다 • get tripped up: 넘어지다, 실수하다 • unforeseen: 예상치 못한

66

Eat to live and not live to eat.

Eating a little too much is eating much too much, right? Greedy eaters dig their graves with their teeth. BTW, "Work to live and not live to work" could be a good reminder to workaholics.

• greedy: 욕심 많은 • grave: 무덤 • BTW: by the way • reminder: 주의를 환기시키는 말 • workaholic: 일에 중독된 사람

67

In trust is treason.

Always watch your back. Even a trusted friend may betray you. Better known than trusted. Ronald Reagan used to say: Trust, but verify.

• In trust is reason: 믿는 도끼에 발등 찍힌다 • watch X's back: X의 뒤를 보살피다, X를 보호하다 • betray: 배반하다 • Better known than trusted: 신뢰하기 전에 잘 알아 봐야 한다 • Trust, but verify: 신뢰하더라도 반드시 확인하라

68

A cat in gloves catches no mice.

It may not necessarily be a virtue to play it safe and err on the side of caution. "Nothing venture, nothing gain" says it all. Risk takers often hit it big, don't they?

• A cat in gloves catches no mice: 장갑 낀 고양이는 생쥐를 못 잡는다 • play it safe: 안전한 길을 택하다 • err on the side of caution: 조심이 지나쳐 과오를 범하는 일이 있더라도 조심하다 • Nothing venture, nothing gain: 모험하지 않으면 얻는 것이 없다 • say it all: 그런 취지를 잘 나타내고 있다

69

Great boast, small roast.

Braggarts are always full of hot air. "Great braggers, little doers" also makes the point that big talkers may talk the talk but seldom walk the talk.

• Great boast, small roast: 장담이 클수록 내용이 비게 마련이다 • braggart: 허풍선이 • hot air: 허풍 • talk the talk: 말만 하다 • walk the talk: 말에 걸맞는 행동을 하다

70

A fool's bolt may sometimes hit the mark.

Good judgment is anything but the exclusive province of the wise. It must be remembered that a fool's counsel is sometimes worth heeding and thus should not be cavalierly ignored.

• exclusive province of X: 전적으로 X만의 영역 • worth heeding: 귀기울일 만한, be cavalierly ignored: 오만한 태도로 무시해 버리다

71

The apple doesn't fall far from the tree.

Heredity may be destiny. Why else should parents and offspring have so many traits in common? "It runs in the family" also speaks to the power of our genes.

• The apple doesn't fall far from the tree: 자식이 부모를 닮는 유전은 어쩔 수 없다 • heredity: 유전 • destiny: 운명 • offspring: 자식 • trait: 특징 • in common: 공유하는 • It runs in the family: 그것은 가족의 유전적 특징이다

72

Change brings life.

Change often comes with a fresh breath of air. A kindred message finds expression in "Variety is the spice of life." You can indeed use a change to spice up your life.

• Change brings life: 변화를 주면 인생에 활기가 돈다 • kindred: 유사한 • find expression in X: X에 표현되다 • spice up: 흥미를 더하다, 양념을 하다

73

Slander slings stones at itself.

Speaking evil of others is a contemptible thing, especially when it has no foundation in fact. Falsely accusing others will end up hurting the accuser the most.

• Slander slings stones at itself: 비방은 자기자신에게 돌을 던지는 것이다
• speak evil of X: X를 험담하다 • contemptible: 비열한 • have no foundation in fact: 근거가 없다

74

Turn the other cheek.

(Matthew 5:39)

No revenge at all may indeed be the best revenge. We are told here to forgive the wrongdoer even to the point of letting him wrong us again.

• Turn the other cheek: 한쪽 뺨을 때리면 다른 쪽 뺨도 내어 주라 • revenge: 복수 • wrongdoer: (우리에게) 부당한 행동을 하는 사람 • to the point of Xing: X하는 정도까지 • wrong: 부당하게 대하다

75

Shod in the cradle, barefoot in the stubble.

Parental overprotectiveness may do children more harm than good. It may ill prepare them for the rough road of the real world later on in life.

• Shod in the cradle, barefoot in the stubble: (요람에서 지내던) 어린 시절 신발을 신고 자라면 자라서 (험한) 그루터기 위를 맨발로 다니게 된다 • parental overprotectiveness: 부모의 과잉 보호 • rough: 험한

76

He has nothing that is not contented.

How rich or poor we feel has little to do with how much we actually have. Rather, it's a function of how contented we are with what is already in our possession.

• have little to do with X: X와 관계가 거의 없다 • function of X: X의 산물/결과
• in X's possession: possessed by X

77

March borrowed from April three days, and they were ill.

This proverb speaks to typical March weather being on the cold and blustery side. March indeed comes in with adder heads and does not necessarily go out with peacock tails.

• be on the cold and blustery side: 춥고 바람이 거센 편이다 • with adder heads: 독사 머리를 하고, 혹독하게 • with peacock tails: 공작 꼬리를 하고, 온화하게

78

Evil doers are evil dreaders.

Bad people are always quick to suspect other people. They tend to think that other people are all as evil-minded and thus evil-prone as they themselves are.

• Evil doers are evil dreaders: 나쁜 짓을 하는 사람은 남이 자신에게 나쁜 짓을 할까 두려워한다 • quick to suspect: 쉽게 의심하다 • evil-minded: 마음이 나쁜 • evil-prone: 나쁜 짓을 하는 성향이 있는

79

Love me, love my dog.

If you truly love me, that love should extend to all those near and dear to my heart as well. Your love for me alone just doesn't suffice.

• Love me, love my dog: 나를 사랑하거든 내 개까지도 사랑해 다오 • extend to X: X에게 까지도 확대 적용되다 • near and dear to my heart: 내가 소중히 여기는 • not suffice: 충분치 못 하다

80

Every dog has his day.

Fortune has a way of smiling upon everybody one day or another. Thus nobody can be dismissed as hopeless no matter how grim things may get for them.

• Every dog has his day: 쥐구멍에도 볕 들 날이 있다 • smile upon X: X에게 미소 짓다 • dismiss X as hopeless: X를 별 볼일 없는 것으로 치부하다 • grim: 모진, 절망적인

81

Union is strength.

Strength emanates from solidarity. United, even weak things become strong. Rooted in the spirit of this message is the motto "One for all and all for one."

• Union is strength: 단합이 힘이다 • emanate from X: X로 부터 나오다
• united: 단결하면 • rooted in X: X에 근거를 둔 • One for all and all for one: 개인은 전체를 위하고, 전체는 개인을 위하여 (행동한다)

82

The absent are always in the wrong.

It's always easy to lay the blame for everything at the door of the absent. They thus tend to end up getting a raw deal. The absent saint gets no candle, does (s)he ever?

• The absent are always in the wrong: 잘못은 항시 현장에 없는 사람 몫이다
• lay the blame for X at the door of Y: X에 대한 잘못이 Y에 있는 것으로 치부하다 • get a raw deal: 부당한 대우를 받다

83

Hard words break no bones.

A reproach does sting. It can do us a world of good, though, especially when it comes from those who really care about us.

• Hard words break no bones: 호된 꾸지람이 뼈를 부러뜨리지는 않는다
• reproach: 질책 • sting: (톡 쏘듯이) 아프다 • a world of X: 매우 많은 X
• care about X: X를 염려하다

84

A black hen lays a white egg.

Anything but infallible, human perception is often misleading. What you see isn't always what you get. Things are not always what they seem, as they say.

• A black hen lays a white egg: 까만 닭이 하얀 알을 낳는다 • infallible: 잘못에서 자유로운 • perception: 인식 • misleading: 잘못된 • What you see is/isn't what you get: 속과 겉이 같다/다르다

85

Gifts blind all eyes.

Not many people are impervious to bribery. That said, we must watch out for the insidious approach of bribes often masquerading as mere gifts.

• Gifts blind all eyes: 선물을 받으면 모두 눈이 멀게 된다 • impervious to X: X의 영향에서 자유로운 • watch out for X: X를 경계하다 • insidious approach: 눈치 채지 못하는 가운데 슬그머니 다가옴 • masquerade as X: X로 가장하다

86

He that hurts another hurts himself.

Whoever contemplates harming others would do well to think twice. Cruelty has a way of coming home to roost. Like a boomerang, the deed often comes back upon the doer.

• contemplate X: X를 고려하다 • would do well to do X: X하는 것이 현명할 것이다 • think twice: 재고하다 • come home to roost: 그 대가를 치르게 하다 • The deed comes back upon the doer: 잘못을 저지르면 그 대가를 치르게 된다

87

After the feast comes the reckoning.

More often than not, pleasure comes with a sting in its tail. The greater the pleasure, the sharper the sting. Which should give all pleasure seekers pause for thought.

• After the feast comes the reckoning: 연회가 끝나면 비용처리를 해야 한다 • Pleasure comes with a sting in its tail: 쾌락은 그 꼬리에 아픈 "독침"이 들어 있다 • pause for thought: 한 번 생각하는 계기

88

Life is no bed of roses.

Who said life is all fun and games? Life often throws at us tough things to deal with, doesn't it? It is thus our lot to take the rough with the smooth.

• Life is no bed of roses: 인생은 장미화단(편안한 침대)만은 아니다 • not all fun and games: 모두 즐겁고 유쾌한 것만은 아닌 • throw at us things to deal with: 우리들에게 풀어야 할 문제들을 안겨 주다 • take the rough with the smooth: 때로는 좋은 일을 겪고 때로는 나쁜 일을 겪다

89

Fine feathers make fine birds.

How a bird looks is a function of the feathers it has on. By the same token, our apparel can affect our looks. Which lies at the root of our fashion-consciousness.

• Fine feathers make fine birds: 예쁜 깃털이 예쁜 새를 만든다 • a function of X: X의 산물/결과 • the feather it has on: 그것의 깃털 / 그것이 '입고 있는' 깃털 • by the same token: 마찬가지로 • fashion-consciousness: 패션 감각/의식

90

No protection is as sure as innocence.

A clean conscience is the surest shield against any harm or accusation. As long as you haven't done anything wrong, you don't have a thing to worry about.

• No protection is as sure as innocence: 결백함 보다 확실한 보호(장치)는 없다 • clean conscience: 아무 것도 거리낌 없는 깨끗한 양심 • shield against X: X를 막는 방패 • accusation: 비난

91

Fools rush in where angels fear to tread.

(Alexander Pope)

The advice implied here is to hold back from foolhardy action. The wise always look twice before they leap. A quick sentence is the mark of a foolish judge.

• Fools rush in where angels fear to tread: 어리석은 사람들은 천사들이 가기를 두려워하는 곳에 겁 없이 뛰어 든다 • hold back from X: X를 자제하다 • look twice before they leap: 뛰어 들기 전에 신중하게 생각하다

92

A lie is the curse of God.

Telling a lie is as bad as sin. Liars are beneath contempt. They are often as despicable as thieves or even more so. We must thus give all forms of deceit a wide berth.

• curse: 저주 • as bad as sin: very bad, 매우 나쁜 • beneath contempt: 경멸할 가치도 없는 • despicable: 비열한 • give X a wide berth: X를 멀리 하다 • deceit: 속임수

93

A (wo)man in debt is caught in a net.

Debtors are no free agents. They are prisoners to their creditors. Those who treasure their freedom and dignity thus should never let debt touch them in any way.

• A (wo)man in debt is caught in a net: 빚진 사람은 덫에 걸려 있다 • free agent: 얽매임이 없는 자유인 • dignity: 위엄, 존엄 • touch: 영향을 미치다

94

Far from eye, far from heart.

We are likely to forget those who are not in our immediate presence. "Out of sight, out of mind" makes a similar point. Absence can make the heart grow fonder, though.

• Far from eye, far from heart: 눈에서 멀어지면, 가슴/마음에서 멀어진다 • in X's immediate presence: X가 있는 바로 그 곳에 • Absence makes the heart grow fonder: 멀리 떨어져 있으면 보고픔이 더욱 간절해진다

95

Rats desert a sinking ship.

An acid test of loyalty often materializes when an organization falls on hard times. Only rotten apples would leave the distressed outfit in the lurch.

• Rats desert a sinking ship: 쥐들은 침몰하는 배를 버리고 도망친다 • acid test: (진위를 가리는) 혹독한 시험 • materialize: 나타나다 • fall on hard times: 어려운 상황을 당하다 • rotten apple: 저질의 인간 • distressed outfit: 위태로운 처지에 놓인 집단 • lurch: 곤경

96

The bigger they are, the harder they fall.

Bigger may not necessarily be better. The higher up the social ladder we climb, for example, the greater tends to be the danger that we get exposed to.

• The bigger they are, the harder they fall: 거물일수록 추락(의 충격)도 크다
• the higher up the social ladder we climb: 우리의 사회적 지위가 높아질수록
• get exposed to X: X에 노출되다

97

He who hesitates is lost.

Making something great happen is not for the faint of heart. When fortune smiles, embrace her without the least hesitation. Remember that the present is never present for long.

• He who hesitates is lost: 주저하다가는 기회를 놓친다 • not for the faint of heart: 마음 약한 사람들은 감당할 수 없는 • without the least hesitation: 조금도 주저함이 없이 • The present is never present for long: 현재는 곧 지나가 버린다

98

Nothing hurts like the truth.

"The sting of a reproach is in the truth of it" says it all, doesn't it? Oh, and they say that truth finds foes where it makes none.

• Nothing hurts like the truth: 진실처럼 뼈아픈 것은 없다 • The sting of a reproach is in the truth of it: 질책이 뼈아픈 것은 그것이 사실에 뿌리를 두고 있다는 데 있다 • Truth finds foes where it makes none: 진실은 적을 사지 않은 곳에서도 적을 만난다

99

A mother can take care of ten children, but sometimes ten children cannot take care of one mother.

This is a tale of a mother's love being boundless. Children's love for their mothers pales next to that of the latter for the former. Maternal love is so unconditional.

• boundless: 무한한 • pale next to X: X와는 비교도 안 된다 • maternal love: 모정, 어머니의 사랑 • unconditional: 무조건적인

100

Money can't buy happiness.

All happiness is in the mind, right? Admittedly, material well-being may often be a necessary condition for happiness. It is anything but a sufficient condition, however, is it?

• All happiness is in the mind: 모든 행복은 마음속에서 나온다 • admittedly: 솔직히 말해서 • material well-being: 물질적으로 편안함/넉넉함 • necessary/sufficient condition: 필요/충분 조건

101

Spare when you are young, and spend when you are old.

Let's all try and save when young for when we are old. We must all work hard to set aside enough before old age catches up to us. Old age will be upon us before we know it.

• spare: 아끼다 • for when we are old: 우리의 노년기를 위하여 • set aside: 저축하다 • be upon X: X에 다가 와있다 • before we know it: 우리도 모르는 사이에, 어느덧

102

Never let your left hand know what your right hand is doing.

(Matthews 6:3)

Under no circumstances are our good deeds to be worn on our sleeve. Virtue is its own reward. Whatever good we do should be done for its own sake, never for show.

• under no circumstances: 어떠한 경우라도 (안 된다) • wear X on Y's sleeve: Y가 X를 공개적으로 내보이다 • be X's own reward: X 그 자체가 보상이다 • for X's own sake: X 자체를 위하여

103

Old shoes are easiest.

We don't need to break in old shoes, do we? They require no getting used to. Thus we often choose to go with the flow, rather than against it. The status quo tends to be preferred to a new regime.

• Old shoes are easiest: 헌 신발이 가장 편하다 • break in X: X를 길들이다
• get used to X: X에 익숙해지다 • go with the flow: 일반적인 흐름을 따르다, 다른 사람들이 하는 대로 하다 • status quo: 현상

104

Curiosity killed the cat.

Risk-takers may be upended by unforeseen dangers. They also say, however, that a cat in gloves catches no mice. Risk apparently cuts both ways.

• Curiosity killed the cat: 호기심이 고양이를 죽였다 • upend X: X를 넘어뜨리다
• unforeseen: 예상치 못한 • cut both ways: 양면성이 있다, 좋기도 하고 나쁘기도 하다

105

It takes all kinds of people to make a world.

Our fellow earthlings can be quite different from ourselves. And this enriches our planet quite a bit. Diverse is indeed so beautiful that intolerance seldom has any leg to stand on.

• earthling: 지구인, 인간 • enrich: 풍요롭게 하다 • quite a bit: to a fairly large extent, 아주 많이 • intolerance: 편협, 관용을 베풀지 못함 • not have a leg to stand on: 정당성이 결여되다

106

Weeds want no sowing.

"Rotten apples" have a way of turning up everywhere. "Bad eggs" are found all over the place without anyone doing anything for them to be there.

• Weeds want no sowing: 잡초는 씨를 뿌리지 않아도 저절로 난다 • rotten apple: 나쁜 사람 • have a way of Xing: X하는 습성이 있다 • turn up: 나타나다 • bad egg: bad apple, rotten apple

107

An empty sack cannot stand upright.

The poor cannot always afford to keep on the straight and narrow. They may sometimes have to bend rather than break. Matters of survival may take precedence over strict moral standards.

• An empty sack cannot stand upright: 빈 자루는 (똑) 바로 설 수 없다 • keep on the straight and narrow: 올곧은 길을 가다, 도덕적 정도를 가다 • bend rather than break: 부러지기 보다는 구부러지다 • take precedence over X: X에 우선하다

108

Many would be cowards if they had courage enough.

It is not necessarily a sign of cowardliness to run away from danger. In fact, it often takes a brave heart to do so. Discretion can sometimes trump valor.

• Many would be cowards if they had courage enough: 용기만 있다면 많은 사람들이 겁쟁이가 될 것이다 • discretion: 신중(함) • trump: 이기다 • valor: 용기

109

Desire has no rest.

Always wishing to be on the way up must be very stressful. Desire can be extremely demanding. Ambition hardly ever leaves any room for peace of mind.

• Desire has no rest: 욕망은 휴식이 없다 • on the way up: 오르막 길에 있는, 출세지향적인 • stressful: 스트레스가 싸이는 • demanding: 힘든 • room for peace of mind: 마음의 평화를 위한 여유

110

Murder will out.

Nothing remains a secret forever. It is no use trying to keep something permanently under wraps. Which is especially the case with something ugly. Truth and oil are ever above, right?

• Murder will out: 살인은 밝혀지게 마련이다 • keep X under wraps: X를 숨기다
• Truth and oil are ever above: 진실과 기름은 항시 위로 떠오르게 마련이다

111

The eye is bigger than the belly.

We must always watch out for our appetite. We tend to desire more than is warranted by our ability to digest. We have to keep from biting off more than we can chew.

• The eye is bigger than the belly: 눈이 배보다 크다, 식탐이 양보다 크다 • watch out for X: X를 경계하다 • warrant: 정당화하다 • keep from Xing: X하는 것을 삼가다 • bite off more than one can chew: 자신의 능력 밖의 일을 떠맡다, 자신이 씹을 수 있는 이상의 (먹을) 양을 베어 내다

112

Love thy neighbor as thyself.

(Leviticus 19:18)

A near neighbor is better than a far-dwelling kinsman, right? Neighbors are at least as precious as family and friends. Would life as we know it be imaginable without neighbors?

• A near neighbor is better than a far-dwelling kinsman: (가까이 사는) 이웃이 멀리 있는 친척 보다 낫다 • precious: 소중한 • life as we know it: 우리가 알고 있는 그런 삶

113

Hope for the best, and prepare for the worst.

Always stay upbeat. At the same time, however, reckon with any eventuality and get prepared for the worst. Fortune favors those who are optimistic and ready.

• Hope for the best, and prepare for the worst: 최선을 희망하고 최악에 대비하라 • upbeat: 낙관적인 • reckon with X: X를 고려하다 • eventuality: 만일의 사태 • Fortune favors X: 행운은 X의 편이다

114

Penny wise and pound foolish.

Thrift is not always a virtue. It can sometimes cause us to miss out on things of value. The advice implied here is not to be foolish enough to spare where we must spend.

• Penny wise and pound foolish: 푼 돈은 챙기고 큰 돈은 헤프게 쓰다 • thrift: 절약, 검소 • miss out on X: X를 놓치다 • spare where we must spend: 꼭 써야 할 돈을 아끼다

115

Leave well (enough) alone.

Don't go look for trouble when things are already pretty much under control. Disruptive behavior does nobody any good, does it? "Let sleeping dogs lie" says about the same thing.

• Leave well (enough) alone: 긁어 부스럼내지 말라 • pretty much under control: 꽤 잘 되고 있는 • disruptive: 분열을 초래하는 • Let sleeping dogs lie: 잠사는 개를 건드리지 말리

116

Once bitten, twice shy.

Once bitten by a snake, for example, one learns to steer clear of a place where a snake bite is a distinct possibility. There is no teacher quite like experience, is there?

• Once bitten, twice shy: 한 번 물리면 다음 부터는 피한다 • steer clear of X: X를 피하다 • snake bite: 뱀에 물림 • be a distinct possibility: 분명히 가능한 일 • There is no X quite like Y: Y만큼 좋은 X는 없다

117

He who makes no mistakes makes nothing.

Mistakes are part and parcel of learning to do things in life. Learning to use English is no exception. No one can master the language without making tons of mistakes in the process.

• part and parcel: 필요한 부분 • be no exception: 예외가 아니다 • tons of mistakes: 수없이 많은 오류들 • in the process: 그 과정에서

118

A holy habit cleanses not a foul soul.

A foul soul is a foul soul (is a foul soul) no matter how it is garbed. What's inside is bound to show through however clever the disguise may be.

• A holy habit cleanses not a foul soul: 복장이 성스럽다고 영혼이 깨끗해지는 것은 아니다 • no matter how X is garbed: X가 어떤 복장을 하고 있건 • show through: 드러나다 • disguise: 가장, 변장

119

Man proposes, God disposes.

Always bear in mind that mere human will pales when compared with the will of God. Whether or not you get your wish is up to God. So do your best and let God do the rest.

• Man proposes, God disposes: 인간은 제안만 하고, 결정은 신이 한다 • pale when compared with X: X와 비교하면 초라하다 • be up to X: X에 달려 있다

120

No (wo)man is indispensable.

Nobody is irreplaceable no matter how good they may be at what they do. Job security should thus concern us all. It is worth remembering that our hubris can often be our undoing.

• indispensable: 없어서는 안될 • irreplaceable: 대체할 수 없는 • job security: 직업의 안정 • hubris: 오만 • be X's undoing: X의 파멸을 부르다

121

Anger is a short madness.

Anger drives a person insane albeit just for the duration of that anger. When we grow angry, our reason rides out. No wonder, they say that anger begins with folly and ends with repentance.

• drive X insane: X가 이성을 잃게 하다 • for the duration of X: X가 계속되는 동안 • our reason rides out: 우리의 이성이 실종되다 • folly: 어리석음 • repentance: 후회

122

Keep your mouth shut and your ears open.

The advice here is to hear much and speak little. Maybe it is not for nothing that we all have two ears but just one mouth. Remember: Many words, many buffets.

• Hear much and speak little: 남의 말은 많이 듣고, 자기 말은 조금만 하라
• Many words, many buffets: 말이 많으면, 많이 두들겨 맞게 된다

123

No (wo)man can do two things at once.

Let multitaskers beware. When attention is divided between two things, we are often not able to do justice to either. Split allegiances may not be worth that much after all.

• multitasker: 여러 일을 한꺼번에 하는 사람 • When attention is divided between two things: 주의력이 두 가지 일에 분산되면 • do justice to X: X를 제대로 다루다 • split allegiances: 분산된 충성심/집중력

124

Give credit where credit is due.

We shouldn't be too stingy with compliments, should we? Common decency requires that a job well done be acknowledged whenever one is in evidence no matter who did it.

• Give credit where credit is due: 인정할 것은 인정하라 • stingy with compliments: 칭찬에 인색한 • common decency: 일반적인 예절 • be in evidence: 나타나다

125

A liar is not believed when he tells the truth.

Crying wolf is good for nothing. A(n) habitual liar loses everybody's trust. The occasional truth originating from him or her is likely to be dismissed as just another lie.

• cry wolf: 있지도 않은 위험을 호소하며 도움을 요청하다 • be good for nothing: 아무런 쓸모도 없다 • lose X's trust: X의 신뢰를 잃다 • originate from X: X로부터 나오다 • dismiss as just another lie: 또 다시 거짓말을 하고 있겠지 하고 무시하다

126

A prophet is not without honor save in his own country.

(Matthew 13:57)

A person is often denied the recognition (s)he rightly deserves by those who are (too) close to him or her. Familiarity does seem to breed contempt, doesn't it?

• prophet: 예언자 • save: except, 제외하고는 • familiarity: 친숙함 • breed contempt: 경멸을 낳다

127

Learn not and know not.

There is nothing like learning when it comes to knowledge acquisition. A dwarf on a giant's shoulders sees further of the two. And that is the beauty of having truly great teachers.

• Learn not and know not: 배우지 않으면 알지 못한다 • There is nothing like X: X가 최고다 • acquisition: 습득 • dwarf: 난장이 • see further of the two: 둘 가운데 너 멀리 보디

128

Small chillies are hot.

Small things or persons can punch way above their weight. They often pack a wallop. Never underestimate or disrespect anyone just because they are not big.

• punch way above X's weight: X의 체급을 훨씬 뛰어 넘는 강타력을 갖다
• pack a wallop: 강타력을 갖다 • underestimate: 과소평가하다 • disrespect: 업신여기다

129

Misfortunes hasten age.

Adversity tends to add to wrinkles and gray hairs, doesn't it? No amount of antioxidants can slow or offset this acceleration in aging that misfortunes bring in their wakes.

• Misfortunes hasten age: 불운은 노화를 앞당긴다 • adversity: 역경 • add to wrinkles and gray hairs: 주름살과 흰머리를 증가시킨다 • no amount of antioxidants: 항산화제가 아무리 많아도 • offset: 상쇄하다 • acceleration: 가속 • in X's wake: X의 뒤에 따르는

130

In fair weather, prepare for fowl.

The suggestion here is that we always plan carefully and be ready for any eventuality. "Thatch your roof before the rain begins" says about the same thing.

• In fair weather, prepare for foul: 날씨가 좋을 때 날씨가 나쁠 때를 대비하라
• Thatch your roof before the rain begins: 비가 시작하기 전에 지붕 이엉을 얹어라

131

Dogs bark as they are bred.

The ill-bred behave the way they do because they were brought up that way. This vantage point seems to cast light on "Birth is much, but breeding is more."

• Dogs bark as they are bred: 개들은 자신들이 배운 대로 짖는다 • ill-bred: 버릇없이 자란 • be brought up that way: 그렇게 양육되다 • vantage point: (잘 보이는) 시각 • cast light on X: X를 조명/설명하다

132

You can't get a quart into a pint.

The point here is that it makes no sense to push our luck when faced with something insurmountable. There is no putting a lake into a mere bucket, for example, is there?

• You can't get a quart into a pint: 콰트를 파인트에 넣을 수 없다 • quart: 4분의 1 갈론 • pint: quart의 8분의 1 • when faced with something insurmountable: 극복할 수 없는 문제에 봉착했을 때에 • There is no putting a lake into a bucket: 호수를 양동이에 담을 수 없다

Key-word Index

(The reference is to the proverb number)

초판 1쇄 인쇄 2011년 8월 8일
초판 1쇄 발행 2011년 8월 15일

지은이 | 박남식
펴낸이 | 박남식
펴낸곳 | 국제영어대학원대학교 출판부
등록 | 2003년 8월 28일(제 17-362호)
주소 | 서울특별시 강동구 성내3동 449-11
전화 | (02) 6477-5105
팩스 | (02) 6477-5111
이메일 | press@igse.ac.kr
홈페이지 | www.igse.ac.kr
ISBN 978-89-956324-6-8 04740
978-89-956324-7-5 04740(전4권)

* 책 값은 뒤표지에 있습니다.